HALF-LIVES

ALSO BY ERICA JONG

FRUITS & VEGETABLES
(poetry)

HALF-LIVES

ERICA JONG

HOLT, RINEHART AND WINSTON

NEW YORK   CHICAGO   SAN FRANCISCO

*Library of Congress Catalog Number: 72-11067
ISBN (Hardbound): 0-03-007426-6
ISBN (Paperback): 0-03-007411-8*
FIRST EDITION
*Designer: Betty Binns
Printed in the United States of America*

Some of these poems originally appeared in the following magazines whose editors are thanked for permission to reprint:

American Poetry Review: "Three Sisters," "Gardener," "In the Skull," "Half-Life"

Aphra: "The Send-Off"

Columbia Forum: "To the Reader," "The Woman Who Loved to Cook"

Cosomopolitan: "Touch," "Purification"

Harper's: "Back to Africa"

Mademoiselle: "Eve on Riverside Drive"

Modern Poetry Studies: "The End of the World"

Ms.: "Paper Cuts," "Mother," "Gardener"

The Nation: "Seventeen Warnings in Search of a Feminist Poem," "Hook," "Anniversary"

New York Quarterly: "Men," "The Eggplant Epithalamion"

Paris Review: "From the Country of Regrets"

Poetry: "Climbing You," "The Universal Explicator," "The Wives of Mafiosi," "The Man Who Can Only Paint Death," "Seminar"

Stooge: "The Bait," "Babyfood"

"The Eggplant Epithalamion" and "Won Ton Soup" first appeared in book form in . . . *And Be Merry,* ed. William Cole, Grossman, 1972.

Grateful acknowledgment is made for use of the following:
One line from "Apprehensions" by Sylvia Plath, from *Crossing*

I am grateful to the Creative Artists Public Service Program of the New York State Council on the Arts, and to the Poetry Society of America for grants which helped in the completion of this book.

Thanks also to Grace Darling Griffin, Patricia Goedicke Robinson, Robert Phillips, Aaron Asher, Norma Klein, Rosellen Brown, Anita Gross, and Louis Untermeyer. Thanks especially to Allan.

FOR MY MOTHER & FATHER

CONTENTS

PROLOGUE / *The Evidence*

I / THE WIVES OF MAFIOSI

Climbing You 11
Seventeen Warnings in
  Search of a Feminist Poem 12
The Wives of Mafiosi 14
Anniversary 15
Divorce 16
Paper Cuts 18
Why I Died 20
How You Get Born 22
Babyfood 23
Men 24
Alcestis on the Poetry Circuit 25
The Critics 27
Three Sisters 28
The Man Who Can Only Paint Death 29
The Widower 30
Back to Africa 31
Mother 33
The Girl in the Mirror 36
Regret 39

II / A CRAZY SALAD

The Eggplant Epithalamion 43
The Woman Who Loved to Cook 46
The Bait 48
Chinese Food 50

On the Air 54
The Send-Off 56
Orphan 61
The Nose 63
Castration of the Pen 66

III / THE AGE OF EXPLORATION

Autobiographical 71
The Age of Exploration 72
Half-Life 74
Knives 76
The Tongue 77
Touch 79
The Cabala According to Thomas Alva Edison 81
Paper Chains 82
Gardener 83
Going to School in Bed 85
The Book with Four Backs 86
Going Away 87
Going Between 89
The Purification 90
Eve on Riverside Drive 91
Sadder 93
Sleeptalk 95
Hook 96
Three 97
For a Marriage 99

IV / SLEEPING WITH DEATH

The Prisoner 103
The Lure of the Open Window 105
In the Skull 106
Thirteen Lines for a Childless Couple 107

The End of the World 108
Waiting 110
Seminar 111
The Universal Explicator 112
The Other Side of the Page 113
From the Country of Regrets 115
To the Reader 127

The notion of emptiness generates passion.
THEODORE ROETHKE

PROLOGUE / The Evidence

1

Evidence of life:
snapshots,
hundreds of split-seconds
when the eyes glazed over,
the hair stopped its growing,
the nails froze in fingertips,
the blood hung suspended
in its vessels—

while the small bloodships,
the red & white bloodboats
buoyed up & down at anchor
like the toys
of millionaires. . . .

Evidence of life:
a split-second's death
to live forever
in something called
a *print*.
A paparazzo life:
I shoot therefore I am.

2

Why does life need evidence
of life?
We disbelieve it
even as we live.

The bloodboats gently rocking,
the skull opening every night
to dreams more vivid than itself,
more solid
than its own bones,
the brain flowering with petals,
stamens, pistils,
magical fruit
which reproduces
from its own juice,
which invents
its own mouth,
& makes itself anew
each night.

3

Evidence of life?
My dreams.
The dreams which I write down.
The dreams which I relate
each morning with a solemn face
inventing as I go.

Evidence of life:
that we could meet for the first time,
open our scars & stitches to each other,
weave our legs around
each other's patchwork dreams

& try to salve each other's wounds
with love—

if it was love.

(I am not sure at all
if love is salve
or just
a deeper kind of wound.
I do not think it matters.)

If it was lust or hunger
& not love,
if it was all that they accused us of
(that we accused ourselves)—
I do not think it matters.

4

Evidence of love?
I imagine our two heads
sliced open like grapefruits,
pressed each half to half
& mingling acid juice
in search of sweet.

I imagine all my dreams
sliding out into your open skull—
as if I were the poet,
you the reader.

I imagine all your dreams
pressed against my belly
like your sperm
& singing into me.

I imagine my two hands
cupped around your life
& stroking it.

I imagine your two hands
making whirlpools
in my blood,
then quelling them.

5

I have no photograph of you.
At times I hardly can believe in you.
Except this ache,
this longing in my gut,
this emptiness which theorizes you
because if there is emptiness this deep,
there must be fullness somewhere.

My other half!
My life beyond this half-life!

Is life a wound
which dreams of being healed?

Is love a wound which deepens
as it dreams?

Do you exist?
Evidence:
these poems in which
I have been conjuring you,
this book which makes your absence palpable,
these longings printed black.

I am exposed.
I am a print of darkness
on a square of film.
I am a garbled dream
told by a breakfast-table liar.
I am a wound which has forgotten how to heal.

6

& if it wasn't love,
if you called me now
across the old echo chamber of the ocean
& said:
"Look, I never loved you,"
I would feel
a little like a fool perhaps,
& yet it wouldn't matter.

My business is to always feel
a little like a fool
& speak of it.

& I am sure
that when we love
we are better than ourselves
& when we hate,
worse.

& even if we call it madness later
& scrawl four-letter words
across those outhouse walls
we call our skulls—
we stand revealed

by those sudden moments
when we come together.

7

Evidence?
Or was it just my dream
waltzing with your dream?
My nightmare kissing yours?

When I awakened
did I walk with Jacob's limp?
Did I sing a different song?
Did I find the inside of my palm
scarred as if
(for moments) it held fire?
Did my blood flow as riverwater flows
around a tree stump—
crooked, with a lilt?

What other evidence
did I need?

I / THE WIVES OF MAFIOSI

*Two habits have taught me how to keep
back my tears: the habit of concealing
my thoughts, and that of darkening my
lashes with mascara.*

COLETTE

*I have to thank God I'm a woman
for in these ordered days a woman only
is free to be very hungry, very lonely.*

ANNA WICKHAM

*(She died of internal
weeping.)*

ELEANOR ROSS TAYLOR

I want to understand the steep thing
that climbs ladders in your throat.
I can't make sense of you.
Everywhere I look you're there—
a vast landmark, a volcano
poking its head through the clouds,
Gulliver sprawled across Lilliput.

I climb into your eyes, looking.
The pupils are black painted stage flats.
They can be pulled down like window shades.
I switch on a light in your iris.
Your brain ticks like a bomb.

In your offhand, mocking way
you've invited me into your chest.
Inside: the blur that poses as your heart.
I'm supposed to go in with a torch
or maybe hot water bottles
& defrost it by hand
as one defrosts an old refrigerator.
It will shudder & sigh
(the icebox to the insomniac).

Oh there's nothing like love between us.
You're the mountain, I am climbing you.
If I fall, you won't be all to blame,
but you'll wait years maybe
for the next doomed expedition.

Seventeen Warnings in Search
of a Feminist Poem

FOR AARON ASHER

1 Beware of the man who denounces ambition;
        his fingers itch under his gloves.

2 Beware of the man who denounces war
        through clenched teeth.

3 Beware of the man who denounces women writers;
        his penis is tiny & cannot spell.

4 Beware of the man who wants to protect you;
        he will protect you from everything but himself.

5 Beware of the man who loves to cook;
        he will fill your kitchen with greasy pots.

6 Beware of the man who loves your soul;
        he is a bullshitter.

7 Beware of the man who denounces his mother;
        he is a son of a bitch.

8 Beware of the man who spells son of a bitch as one word;
        he is a hack.

9 Beware of the man who loves death too well;
        he is taking out insurance.

10 Beware of the man who loves life too well;
        he is a fool.

12

11   Beware of the man who denounces psychiatrists;
            he is afraid.

12   Beware of the man who trusts psychiatrists;
            he is in hock.

13   Beware of the man who picks your dresses;
            he wants to wear them.

14   Beware of the man you think is harmless;
            he will surprise you.

15   Beware of the man who cares for nothing but books;
            he will run like a trickle of ink.

16   Beware of the man who writes flowery love letters;
            he is preparing for years of silence.

17   Beware of the man who praises liberated women;
            he is planning to quit his job.

Thinking to take on the power
   of a dark suit lined with lead
   of a man with a platinum mouth & knuckles of brass
   of a bullet the color of a Ferrari

the wives of Mafiosi stay home
decanting the Chianti
like transparent blood.

They crochet spiders for the furniture.
They go to Confession.
They fill the ears of the priests
with mozzarella & nougat candy.

We too stay home
& dream of power.
   We sacrifice the steakblood to the dishwasher.
   We bring clear offerings of water to the plants.
   We pray before the baby pictures.

We dream of swallowing bullets
& coupling with money.
   We dream of transparent armor.
   We imagine we want peace.
   We imagine we are different
   from the wives of Mafiosi.

Every night for five years
he chewed on her
until her fingers were red & ragged
until blue veins hung out of her legs
until the children tumbled
like baby kangaroos
out of raw crimson pouches
in her stomach.

Now she was done.
She had once been a woman.
She had once sprinkled perfume
from the split ends of her hair.
She had once left a silver trail of sequins
in the moonlight
& slipped between the clouds.
She had once sucked
on inky fingers at school
& drawn a perfect india ink man.
She had once prayed to movie stars & poets.
She had once cried into the *Rubaiyat*.
She had once worshipped swizzle sticks from Birdland
& dreamed of a man with perfect teeth
& a wedding in a carved block of ice.

Eggs boiling in a pot.
They click
like castanets.
I put one in a cup
& slice its head off.

Under the wobbly egg white
is my first husband.
Look how small he's grown
since last we met!

"Eat me," he says agreeably.
I hesitate, then bite.

The thick yolk runs down
my thighs.

I take another egg
& slice its head.
Inside is my second husband.
This one's better done.

"You liked the white," I say,
"I liked the yolk."

He doesn't speak
but scowls as if to say:
"Everyone always eats me
in the end."

I chew him up
but I spit out
his jet-black hair,
the porcelain jackets from his teeth,
his cufflinks, fillings,
eyeglass frames. . . .

I drink my coffee
& I read the *Times*.

Another egg is boiling in the pot.

Endless duplication of lives and objects . . .
THEODORE ROETHKE

I have known the imperial power of secretaries,
the awesome indifference of receptionists,
I have been intimidated by desk & typewriter,
by the silver jaws of the stapler
& the lecherous kiss of the mucilage,
& the unctuousness of rubber cement
before it dries.

I have been afraid of telephones,
have put my mouth to their stale tobacco breath,
have been jarred to terror
by their jangling midnight music,
& their sudden blackness
even when they are white.

I have been afraid in elevators
amid the satin hiss of cables
& the silky lisping of air conditioners
& the helicopter blades of fans.
I have seen time killed in the office jungles
of undeclared war.

My fear has crept into the paper guillotine
& voyaged to the Arctic Circle of the water cooler.
My fear has followed me into the locked Ladies Room,
& down the iron fire stairs
to the postage meter.

I have seen the mailroom women like lost letters
frayed around the edges.
I have seen the xerox room men
shuffling in & out among each other
like cards in identical decks.

I have come to tell you I have survived.
I bring you chains of paperclips instead of emeralds.
I bring you lottery tickets instead of poems.
I bring you mucilage instead of love.

I lay my body out before you on the desk.
I spread my hair amid a maze of rubber stamps.
RUSH. SPECIAL DELIVERY. DO NOT BEND.
I am open—will you lick me like an envelope?
I am bleeding—will you kiss my paper cuts?

She is the woman I follow.
Whenever I enter a room
she has been there—

    with her hair smelling of lions & tigers,
    with her dress blacker than octopus ink,
    with her shoes moving like lizards
    over the waving wheat of the rug.

Sometimes I think of her as my mother
but she died by her own hand
before I was born.

    She drowned in the waves of her own hair.
    She strangled on Isadora's scarf.
    She suckled a poisonous snake at her breast
    like Cleopatra or Eve.

She is no virgin & no madonna.
Her eyelids are purple.
She sleeps around.

    Wherever I go I meet her lovers.
    Wherever I go I hear their stories.
    Wherever I go they tell me
    different versions of her suicide.

I sleep with them in gratitude.
I sleep with them to make them tell.
I sleep with them as punishment or reward.

She is the woman I follow.
I wear her cast-off clothes.
She is my mother, my daughter.
She is writing this suicide note.

One night, your mother is listening to the walls.
The clock whirrs like insect wings.
The ticking says lonely lonely lonely.

In the living room, the black couch swallows her.
She trusts it more than men,
but no one will ever love her
enough.

She doesn't yet know you
so how can she love you?
She loves you like God or Shakespeare.
She loves you like Mozart.

You are trembling in the walls like music.
You cross the ceiling in a phantom car of light.

Meanwhile unborn,
you wait in a heavy rainsoaked cloud
for your father's thunderbolt.
Your mother lies in the living room dreaming your hands.
Your mother lies in the living room dreaming your eyes.

She awakens & a shudder shakes her teeth.
The world is beginning again after the flood.

She slides into bed beside that gray-faced man,
your father.
She opens her legs to your coming.

They made the child so they could touch each other.

His breasts grew round, his belly swelled,
her navel sent a vine to meet his own,
& they took root in each other.

''We are pregnant,'' they would say,
talking to friends.

& she would pat his belly
& pull in her own.

Between his father's legs
the child first saw the world.
It was mountainous & cold.

The women marched together
carrying guns.
The men stayed home & wept.

Now his breasts give milk,
his tears turn into food.
The child is fed on tears just as before.

They made the child to open doors into themselves.

They closed them.
They fed him milk & tears.

(after a poem called "Women" by Nicanor Parra)

The impossible man
The man with the ebony penis ten feet tall
The man of pentelikon marble
The man with the veined bronze figleaf which comes unhinged
The man who's afraid to get pregnant
The man who screws in his socks
The man who screws in his glasses
The man who screws in his sunglasses
The man who gets married a virgin
The man who marries a virgin
The man who wilts out of guilt
The man who adores his mother
The man who makes it with fruit
The husband who never has time
The husband who'd rather have power
The poet who'd rather have boys
The conductor who loves his baton
The analyst who writes "poems"
All these Adonises
All these respectable gents
Those descended
& those undescended
will drive me out of my skull sooner or later

Alcestis on the Poetry Circuit
(*In Memoriam* MARINA TSVETAYEVA,
ANNA WICKHAM, SYLVIA PLATH, SHAKESPEARE'S
SISTER, ETC., ETC.)

The best slave
does not need to be beaten.
She beats herself.

Not with a leather whip,
or with sticks or twigs,
not with a blackjack
or a billyclub,
but with the fine whip
of her own tongue
& the subtle beating
of her mind
against her mind.

For who can hate her half so well
as she hates herself?
& who can match the finesse
of her self-abuse?

Years of training
are required for this.
Twenty years
of subtle self-indulgence,
self-denial;
until the subject
thinks herself a queen
& yet a beggar—
both at the same time.
She must doubt herself
in everything but love.

She must choose passionately
& badly.
She must feel lost as a dog
without her master.
She must refer all moral questions
to her mirror.
She must fall in love with a cossack
or a poet.

She must never go out of the house
unless veiled in paint.
She must wear tight shoes
so she always remembers her bondage.
She must never forget
she is rooted in the ground.

Though she is quick to learn
& admittedly clever,
her natural doubt of herself
should make her so weak
that she dabbles brilliantly
in half a dozen talents
& thus embellishes
but does not change
our life.

If she's an artist
& comes close to genius,
the very fact of her gift
should cause her such pain
that she will take her own life
rather than best us.

& after she dies, we will cry
& make her a saint.

The Critics

(FOR EVERYONE WHO WRITES ABOUT
SYLVIA PLATH INCLUDING ME)

Because she was clamped in the vise of herself
because she was numb
because words moved slowly as glaciers
because they flowed from her mouth like wine
because she was angry
& knotted her hair
& wore sand in her bra
because she had written herself into a corner
& could not get out
because she had painted the sun on her ceiling
& then got burned
because she invented the stars
& watched them fall . . .

There is nothing to say now.
You have filled her grave with your theories,
her eyes with your sights.
You have picked her bones clean
as ancestor bones.
They could not gleam whiter.
But she is gone.
She is grass you have trod.
She is dust you have blown away.

She sits in her book like an aphid,
small & white.
She is patient.
When you're silent
she'll crawl out.

They will never get to Moscow.
They sit on a brown hilltop dangling their feet
into the blue pages of the sky.

One can't stand a house without a baby.
One is handcuffed to a typewriter.
The youngest sits in the center chiding the clouds.

Here is the inside of the dream bus.
The walls are made of clouds that look like glass.
Each in her own way has tried to get in.
But the way was blocked
by quarrels, baby bottles, charge accounts of guilt
& the sour smell of money.

The one with the typewriter rattles her chains & handcuffs.
If only they'd leap onto the keys (she thinks)
they'd learn to dance
If only they'd wrap themselves in dust-jackets
before they die.

The oldest delivers her fourth baby into the sky.
The youngest blames the sky.

The Man Who Can Only Paint Death

A man who does not believe in women
believes in death.
He has painted it rising with bone wings
over the dark of his house.
He has sung to it in a pale monotone.
He has stroked its hair.

But his hand comes back covered with cobwebs
& his throat fills with dust.
The bone wings creak when he raises his brush.
His wife turns in her bed.

He dreams of his mother's grave going to seed.
He smells the dust of her hair.
He is the gray flower which grows
between her headstone & the sky.
He is the weed in the paving crack.
He is the baby in black.

His daughter turns & turns in her sleep.
Her eyelids move with dreams.
She dreams she awakens & finds him gone,
& her grandmother's name is death.

She left him in death's egg,
the bone sack & the gunny sack,
the bag of down & feathers—all black. . . .
Somehow he couldn't get back.

It was night,
a night of shark-faced jets
winking brighter than blue stars,
a night of poisoned cities
mushrooming beneath the eyes of jets,
a night of missile silos
sulking in the desert,
a night of babies howling in the alleys,
a night of cats.

She left a death so huge
his life got lost in it.
She left a bloodstained egg
he had to hatch.

Among the Gallas, when a woman grows tired
of the cares of housekeeping, she begins to
talk incoherently and demean herself extravagantly.
This is a sign of the descent of the holy spirit
Callo upon her. Immediately, her husband prostrates
himself and adores her; she ceases to bear the humble
title of wife and is called "Lord"; domestic duties
have no further claim on her, and her will is a divine law.

SIR JAMES GEORGE FRAZER,
The Golden Bough

Seeing me weary
> of patching the thatch
> of pounding the bread
> of pacing the floor nightly
> with the baby in my arms,

my tall black husband
> (with eyes like coconuts)
> has fallen down on the floor to adore me!
> I curse myself for being born a woman.
> He thinks I'm God!

I mutter incoherently of Friedan, Millett, Freud. . . .
> He thinks the spirit
> has descended.
> He calls me "Lord."

Lord, lord, he's weary in his castle now.
> It's no fun living with a God.
> He rocks the baby, patches thatch

31

& pounds the bread.
I stay out all night with the Spirit.

Towards morning when the Spirit brings me home,
    he's almost too pooped to adore me.
    I lecture him on the nature
    & duties of men.
    ''Biology is destiny,'' I say.

Already I hear stirrings of dissent.
    He says he could have been a movie star.
    He says he needs a full-time maid.
    He says he never *meant*
    to marry God.

Ash falls on the roof
of my house.

I have cursed you enough
in the lines of my poems
& between them,
in the silences which fall
like ash-flakes
on the watertank
from a smog-bound sky.

I have cursed you
because I remember
the smell of *Joy*
on a sealskin coat
& because I feel
more abandoned than a baby seal
on an ice floe red
with its mother's blood.

I have cursed you
as I walked & prayed
on a concrete terrace
high above the street
because whatever I pulled down
with my bruised hand
from the bruising sky,
whatever lovely plum
came to my mouth
you envied
& spat out.

Because you saw me in your image,
because you favored me,
you punished me.

It was only a form of you
my poems were seeking.
Neither of us knew.

For years
we lived together
in a single skin.

We shared fur coats.
We hated each other
as the soul hates the body
for being weak,
as the mind hates the stomach
for needing food,
as one lover hates the other.

I kicked
in the pouch of your theories
like a baby kangaroo.

I believed you
on Marx, on Darwin,
on Tolstoy & Shaw.
I said I loved Pushkin
(you loved him).
I vowed Monet
was better than Bosch.

Who cared?

I would have said nonsense
to please you
& frequently did.

This took the form,
of course,
of fighting you.

We fought so gorgeously!

We fought like one boxer
& his punching bag.
We fought like mismatched twins.
We fought like the secret sharer
& his shade.

Now we're apart.
Time doesn't heal
the baby to the womb.
Separateness is real
& keeps on growing.

One by one the mothers
drop away,
the lovers leave,
the babies outgrow clothes.

Some get insomnia—
the poet's disease—
& sit up nights
nursing
at the nipples
of their pens.

I have made hot milk
& kissed you where you are.
I have cursed my curses.
I have cleared the air.
& now I sit here writing,
breathing you.

Throwing away my youth on duty
        on ink, on guilt,
        on applications . . .

I thought of you
        in your mirrored room,
        you with the huge open heart
        pulsing like a womb which has just given birth,
        pulsing like the beat in my head
        before a poem starts.

I thought of you
        & your charmed life,
        your hassocks, waterbeds & sliding mirrors,
        your closets full of beautiful faces,
        & your men, your men

the way you could open & close
        your legs without guilt,
        the way you said yes & yes & yes,
        the way you dealt death & regret
        as if they were cards,
        the way you asked nothing
        & everything came to you

Remember how we both loved
        that girl from the Kingdom of Oz? *

36

She had thirty heads—all beautiful—
        but just one dress.

She kept her heads in a mirrored cupboard
        opened with a ruby key.
        It was chained to her wrist.

She had my heart chained to her wrist!
        I wanted to *be* her.

Though some of her heads were mad
        she could never remember which
        until she wore them,
        & one had a terrible temper,
        & one loved blood.

Can you imagine a girl
        who put on the wrong head one day
        & killed her body by mistake?

Can you imagine a girl
        who would not believe she was beautiful
        & kept opening her legs to the wrong men?

Can you imagine a girl
        who cut off her head
        to get rid of the guilt?

But no:
        you are lying in a room
        where everything is silver.
        The ceiling is mirrored,
        the floor is mirrored,
        & men come out of the walls.

One by one, they make love to you
   like princes climbing a glass mountain.
   They admire your faces
   & the several colors of your hair.
   They admire your smooth pink feet
   & your hands which have never known ink.
   They kiss your fingers.

You are everywhere.
   You can come all night
   & never tire.

Your voices mist the mirrors
   but you never write.

You have my children
   & they fugue the world.

Someday when my work is done
   I'll come to you.

No one will be the wiser.

* Princess Langwidere in L. Frank Baum's *Ozma of Oz*.

Regret

FOR MIMI BAILIN

Regret is the young girl who sits in the snow
& stares at her hands.

They are bluer than shadows in snow.
They are bloodless as fear.
Her fingernail moons are white.

She wants to crawl into the palm
of her own hand.
She wants extra fingers to cover
the shame of her eyes.

She wants to follow her lifeline where it leads
but it plunges deeper
than the Grand Canyon.

She stands on the edge
still hoping
she can fly.

II / A CRAZY SALAD

It's certain that fine women eat
A crazy salad with their meat
Whereby the horn of plenty is undone.
WILLIAM BUTLER YEATS

Even his heart wishes to bite apples.
THEODORE ROETHKE

The Eggplant Epithalamion
FOR GRACE & DAVID GRIFFIN

"Mostly you eat eggplant at least once a day," she
explained. *"A Turk won't marry a woman unless
she can cook eggplant at least a hundred ways."*
ARCHAEOLOGIST IRIS LOVE, SPEAKING OF THE CUISINE ON
DIGS IN TURKEY. *The New York Times,* February 4, 1971

1

There are more than a hundred Turkish poems
about eggplant.
I would like to give you all of them.
If you scoop out every seed,
you can read me backward
like an Arabic book.
Look.

2

(Lament in Aubergine)

Oh aubergine,
egg-shaped
& as shiny as if freshly laid—
you are a melancholy fruit.
Solanum Melongena.
Every animal is sad
after eggplant.

3

(Byzantine Eggplant Fable)

Once upon a time on the coast of Turkey
there lived a woman who could cook eggplant 99 ways.

She could slice eggplant thin as paper.
She could write poems on it & batter-fry it.
She could bake eggplant & broil it.
She could even roll the seeds in banana-
flavored cigarette papers
& get her husband high on eggplant.
But he was not pleased.
He went to her father & demanded his bride-price back.
He said he'd been cheated.

He wanted back two goats, twelve chickens
& a camel as reparation.
His wife wept & wept.
Her father raved.

The next day she gave birth to an eggplant.
It was premature & green
& she had to sit on it for days
before it hatched.
"This is my hundredth eggplant recipe," she screamed.
"I hope you're satisfied!"

(Thank Allah that the eggplant was a boy.)

4

(*Love & the Eggplant*)

On the warm coast of Turkey, Miss Love
eats eggplant
"at least once a day."

How fitting that love should eat eggplant,
that most aphrodisiac fruit.

Fruit of the womb
of Asia Minor,
reminiscent of eggs,
of Istanbul's deep purple nights
& the Byzantine eyes of Christ.

I remember the borders of egg & dart
fencing us off from the flowers & fruit
of antiquity.
I remember the egg & tongue
probing the lost scrolls of love.
I remember the ancient faces
of Aphrodite
hidden by dust
in the labyrinth under
the British Museum
to be finally found by Miss Love
right there
near Great Russell Square.

I think of the hundreds of poems of the eggplant
& my friends who have fallen in love
over an eggplant,
who have opened the eggplant together
& swum in its seeds,
who have clung in the egg of the eggplant
& have rocked to sleep
in love's dark purple boat.

Looking for love, she read cookbooks,
She read recipes for *tartlettes*,
terrines de boeuf, timbales,
& Ratatouille.
She read cheese fondue
& Croque Monsieur,
& Hash High Brownies
& Lo Mein.

If no man appeared who would love her
(her face moist with cooking,
her breasts full of apple juice
or wine),
she would whip one up:
of gingerbread,
with baking powder
to make him rise.

Even her poems
were recipes.
"Hunger," she would write, "hunger."
The magic word to make it go away.
But nothing filled her up
or stopped that thump.
Her stomach thought it was a heart.

Then one day she met a man,
his cheeks brown as gingerbread,
his tongue a slashed pink ham
upon a platter.
She wanted to eat him whole

& save his eyes.
Her friends predicted he'd eat her.

How does the story end?
You know it well.

She's getting fatter
& she drinks too much.

Her shrink has read her book
& heard her tale.

"Oral," he says,
& coughs
& puffs his pipe.

"Oral,"
he says,
& now
"time's up."

The Bait

(WITH APOLOGIES TO SIR WALTER RALEIGH,
CHRISTOPHER MARLOWE,
JOHN DONNE, ET AL.)

The poet of sulks.
I had often seen him at a bar,
or at a reading,
sulking through the smoke.

In his pocket
a manuscript crackled
giving off
an acrid smell.

"If they'd shut up,"
his scowl seemed to say,
"I'd show them all
what poetry's about."

I swear his meanness turned me on.
I took him home.

I fed him rice & shrimps & cheesecake
& white wine.
I tickled his tongue with puns.

The poet of sulks
would have none of this.
He called me trivial
because I like to laugh.

He laid me once & then attacked
my poems & cooking—
which he'd got confused.

"Your cheesecake poem is rather rich,"
he grudged.
"Your rice is overdone."

I saw that I'd get nowhere
with this guy.
So I began to sulk.

After an hour or two
he finally caught on.

"What's bugging you?"
he asked.

"I'm waiting for the sky to fall,"
I gloomed.
"I'm waiting for the Apocalypse
to fuck me from behind."

"Do you really think it will?"
he asked.
"I'm sure of it,"
I said.

"Come live with me & be my love," said he.

Chinese Food

The mouth is an unlimited measure.

CHINESE PROVERB

WON TON SOUP

The soup contains something from each moment
of your life.
It is hot & sour.
There are islands of chives floating
like green ideas in the mind.
There is the won ton folded
like an embryo
skimming the water
waiting to be born.
There are the small unkosher bits of pork,
forbidden foods
which promise all the flavor.
There are the crystal noodles :
threads of silver light.

You eat your life
out of a skull-shaped bowl.
You eat it
with a porcelain spoon.
It is dense as water.
It is sour as death.
It is hot as an adulterous love.
& the pork—forbidden both by Moses & Mohammed—
is pink & sweet.

ENTREE

For the next course we chose
1 from Column A
2 from Column B
4 from Column C
& we passed the plates around
to share our lives.

We wanted to say: Look—
you taste my portion,
I'll taste yours.

We wanted to say: Look—
I am dying of malnutrition.
Let's eat each other.

We wanted to say: Look—
I am tired of eating myself
every night
& every morning.
I am frightened
of my own mouth
which wants to devour me.
I am tired of the tapeworms
of my soul.

Belle ordered spareribs
sweet & sour.
"I have given my life to men,"
she said.
Like Eve in the garden
she chewed the rib
& regretted nothing.

Allan ate his beef with oyster sauce
& did not apologize
to Jews or Hindus.
"Sometimes food is only food,"
he said.

Roland ordered vegetables
& crunched
& spoke of meter.

Lucas ordered chicken
& denounced analysis.

Betty ordered dumplings
& defended it.

While Neal & Susan
dug deep
into their noodles.

I was left with sweet & sour pork,
haloed in batter,
glowing red with sauce,
slick as guilt
& sweet as smashed taboos.

Then we all poured tea.

FORTUNE COOKIES

The man who chews on his woman
will be poisoned by her gall.

The woman who chews on her man
will end her days as a toothless hag.

The poet who writes of food
will never go hungry.

The poet who describes her friends at table
will eat her words.

The poet who writes on rice paper
will nourish her critics.

A poem about food will not feed
the starving nations.

Your own mouth will eat you
if you don't watch out.

[*He*] *went entirely mad and had the delusion his penis was a radio station.* . . .

THEODORE ROETHKE IN CLASS, QUOTED
BY ALLAN SEAGER IN *The Glass House*

One toe
is the sensitive tip
of an iceberg,
& the moon sets
in my pinkie nail.
Every hair on my head
is transmitting signals.
My nipples give off
ultrasonic bleeps.

Only mad dogs
& lovers hear them.
Only distant poets
who are wired for sound.
He thinks his heart
is a receiving station.
His penis keeps on playing Rock & Roll.

I love a lunatic
whose feet are stereophonic.
His moustache tingles
like a tuning fork.
His fingers jangle
like a snail's antennae.
His navel rotates
like a radar screen.

Do you read me? Do you read me?
I keep asking.
When we're apart, when we're together
I keep asking.
& all the time he's spinning golden oldies.
His balls play Dixieland.
His foreskin honky tonk.

I play the engineer to his disk jockey.
I signal him to take a station break.
I ask him to identify the network.
I tell him to stop censoring the news.

It's Rock & Roll & Soul
& Body Counts.
It's pimple cream & soda pop
& jazz.
He thinks the FCC
has got his number.
He blames the President
when signals come in weak.
He thinks J. Edgar Hoover
sends him static.
& when he wilts,
he blames the FBI.

FOR PATRICIA GOEDICKE & LEONARD ROBINSON

(A letter to friends after sending the first book to the printer)

1

(Singing the Monthly Blues)

The book gone to the printer to die
& the flat-bellied author
disguised as me
is sick of the anger of being a woman
& sick of the hungers
& sick of the confessional poem of the padded bra
& the confessional poem of the tampax
& the bad-girl poets
who menstruate black ink.

I am one!
Born from my father's head
disguised as a daughter
angry at spoons & pots
with a half-life of men behind me
& a half-life of me ahead
with holes in my shoes
& holes in my husbands
& only the monthly flow of ink to keep me sane
& only sex to keep me pure.

I want to write about something other than women!
I want to write about something other than men!
I want stars in my open hand
& a house round as a pumpkin
& children's faces forming in the roots of trees.

2

Instead
I read my fortune in the bloodstains on the sheet.

3

What I wanted was something enormous,
a banyan tree
sinking its roots in the ground,
something green & complex as a trellis
eating the air
& the leaves uncurling their fingers
& the tendrils
reaching out for the wisps of my hair
& breathing the transformation.
To become a tree-girl!
with birds nesting in my navel
& poems sprouting from my fingertips—
but a tree with a voice.

4

I had imagined at least
an underground temple:
the Temple to Juno at Paestum,
the bone-jars & the honey-jars
& sacrifices sweetening the earth.

Instead: this emptiness.
The hollow of the book resounding
like an old well
in a ruined city.
No honey pot,
but another *Story of O*.

5

Sometimes the sentimentalist
says to hell with words
& longs to dig ditches.
She writes of this longing, of course,
& you,
because you are her friends,
write back.

6

She wants to write happiness books
with you—
big black happiness books—
because you tell her the moon's in your shoes
because you've taken off each other's socks
& counted each other's toes
& kissed
the spaces in between
because you fall (giggling)
into each other's books & find
the pages skin
because your laughter's the most serious sound
she's heard in years
because when she hears you making love
across the wall
you're singing
possible possible possible
while she sits here
in her big black book
beating her fists against the covers
loving the way she hates herself
much too much
to stop.

7

Here is the bottom of the pool
where the octopus
feeding on herself
vows to stop talking
about how
she wants to stop talking
about feeding on herself.

8

She is so bored with her notebook.
She has taken to writing in colored inks.
Green nouns. Shocking pink verbs.
Her notebook is a Mardi Gras.
The Rorschach on the sheet is brown.

9

She comes back again & again to this :
sex.
No matter how hard they mock her,
no matter what kind of cunt they call her,
no matter how shocked her father & mother,
caught in their cloud bed,
caught as in a primal scene
choreographed by Disney,
she comes back
to the dance
against death.

10

They are sitting in an office high
above Madison Avenue

speaking earnestly of commas.
He loves the way she uses them :
little hooks
to snare his shirt-tails.
But he proposes, tactfully, one semicolon.
Does he dare ?
"I love your stuff," he says.
Stiff blue pencil, he would fall on her,
revising everything.
Her paper dress tears off
& the layers of poems which are her skins
peel off.

She is a little font of tiny type.
She is ink.
She is that fine black trickle
running out the door.

A dream of rejection
in which you are invited
to only the wrong parties—

& when you arrive
it seems you've forgotten your skin
& your mother is there
showing everyone baby pictures.

You still had your skin then!

Why do you feel like an orphan
flayed alive?

Wherever you go
they admire your smile,
the white teeth of your wisecracks,
the apple-red cheeks of your laugh.

How can they know that you cry into your hair
& mop the floor?
That you sweep the rug with your lashes?
That you lick the soles of your lover's feet
to keep them clean?

You always believe he will leave you.
You are always alone.
Even when he lies over you—
a ship plowing
the iceberg edges of your soul,

you are alone,
& only the hunger of being in love
appeases your hunger.

Oh orphan
casting filaments like Whitman's spider,
sending letters to the world on colored paper,
sending photographs & kisses,
care packages & carbon copies,
onion skin—
the only skin you have.

The Nose
FOR LOUIS UNTERMEYER, WHO KNOWS

Nose thou art sick.
You perch on the face
like a discouraged phallic symbol.
You perch between the eyes
like a boring critic.
You perch above the mouth
like a twitch, a boil, a wart,
& you itch at embarrassing times
like lust.

Gogol knew you for elusiveness—
how, just when we *need* a nose—
pouf!—you disappear
into a snotty handkerchief
or loaf of bread.

Pinocchio, that little wooden prick,
that secret pudding-puller,
that school drop-out,
knew how you grow & grow
like a maypole
making the sheets a tent
for your three-ring circus,
you sad impossible clown

(even great noses—
Cyrano, de Gaulle—
have to play the clown,
cannot escape
the general fate of noses).

63

Starlets & unmarriageable girls
whose noses
are far too nubile
cut them off.
The Freudian squints at this
with his diagnosis:
Proboscus Envy.

Most men
find their noses short
& sneak around the locker room
looking for
different colored noses
in repose.
No happy man
is happy with his nose.

My kingdom for a nose!
cried Hamlet.
(Something was blue in Denmark
besides the cheese.)
Ophelia appeared
offering her lily-white snout,
but Hamlet longed to have his mama
blow his nose
(according to Ernest Jones).

He later perished
from his old friend's sword—
Shakespeare playing it,
as always,
to the hilt.

Tales about noses
are always (you see)
moral.

The nose is a very upright organ.
It gets its nose rubbed in the mud.
It sprouts with pimples
from our adolescent dreams.
It figures in a moral song
on Reindeer.
It speaks
in the Braille of blackheads
of our lust.

& meanwhile *Life*
shows me a gigantic photo
of tiny smell-stalks
like a bed of coral.
The nose is the oldest organ
in the animal kingdom.
The nose is the organ
of memory & desire.
Poets are bloodhounds
tracking with their noses.
The nose is life.
Poor Yorick
has no nose.

The pen is an index finger
which has learned
to give milk
like a breast.

It is curious.
It explores
the cunts of girls.
It explores
& tells.

It is nourishing.
It can suckle babies
with the bluest,
blackest milk.

It is clever,
has an endless store
of anecdotes & fables.

It is logical,
can do research,
can put its tip
against your piglike nose,
can even say
FUCK YOU.

But unlike your finger
or your breast
your pen is fickle.
It writes speeches

for two rival politicians.
It endorses checks
from almost anyone.
It writes bad lines
& writes good ones
without caring
& leaves you
to sort out the mess.

By this time
you have gathered
that the pen's a symbol.

Is it breast?
Or is it penis?

Cut it off!

III / THE AGE OF EXPLORATION

*The human spirit is prey to the most
astounding impulses. Man goes constantly in
fear of himself. His erotic urges terrify
him. The saint turns from the voluptuary
in alarm; she does not know that his
unacknowledgeable passions and her own
are really one.*

GEORGES BATAILLE

*Had we remained together
We could have become a silence.*
YEHUDA AMICHAI

The lover in these poems
is me ;
the doctor,
Love.
He appears
as husband, lover
analyst & muse,
as father, son
& maybe even God
& surely death.

All this is true.

The man you turn to
in the dark
is many men.

This is an open secret
women share
& yet agree to hide
as if
they might then
hide it from themselves.

I will not hide.

I write in the nude.
I name names.
I am I.
The doctor's name is Love.

Sailing into your chest,
the white ship of my body
parts
the sun-struck water
of your skin
the silvery waves
of your hair—

a miracle!
the Red Sea parting for Moses—

& we ride
on a bed high
as the *Queen Mary*
& I straddle
your tall red smokestack
like the ocean wind
moaning
in mid-Atlantic.

All around us
people are waving good-bye.

Your wives bobbing in tiny lifeboats,
your children
riding on singing dolphins,
my mother
reaving the water
in an angry speedboat
& shouting warnings

through a megaphone,
my father
coolly shooting clay pigeons
from the burning deck,
my husband
about to harpoon
a great white whale . . .

Abandon ship !
Abandon ship !

We aren't listening.

Last lovers on the *Titanic,*
galley slaves transfixed
by the master's whip,
Jews in steerage,
Spaniards in search of gold . . .

You are the firehose
on my burning deck,
the radar
in my fog,
the compass
in my starless night. . . .

You are the prow
of Columbus' ship
kissing the lip
of the new world.

The rock I danced on
looked for all the world like the sea.
The sea was stone.

Your eyes were green
as wings of horseflies . . .
almost as unclean.

They buzzed around my head
like my own dreams.
They thickened the air with kisses.

When I was nine,
I used to kiss my pillow
on the mouth
after I'd licked it wet.
How else find out
what ''soul-kiss''
really meant?

''He puts his tongue
into your mouth.''

I was amazed.

& yet our tongues are dancing
on the ocean.

Why does every fucking poem
mention the ocean?

The swell of the great sea mother?
The water babies in their amniotic fluid?
The sea salt taste of blood?

Love, blood—the flood of poems
as life creaks to a close.

The sky narrows to a point
as we make love.

This is a little death,
a pact,
a double suicide of sorts.

& I invent
tidal waves, atomic shocks,
the mushroom cloud of you
above the smoking chasm
that you leave in me.

Radioactive,
dangerous as stone,
you leave me bone dry, lonely in my cave.

I have compared you to atomic war.

& your half-life will linger
when both of us
are gone.

The women he has had are all faces
without eyes.
He has entered them blind
as a cut worm.
He has swum their oceans
like a wounded fish
looking for home.

At nights when he can't sleep,
he dreams of weaving
backward up that river
where the banks
are fringed with mouths,
& weedy hair
grows amid the dark crusts
of ancient blood.

Tonight, he is afraid & lonely
in a city of meat & knives.
I would go under his knife
& move so willingly
that his heart
might turn to butter
in his mouth.

The Tongue

I crouch under your tongue
like a lover afraid
of her own lie.
The tongue is the organ of love
& the organ of lying.
& the lie clings to the tongue;
the lie fills
the hungry mouth of the world.

I remember the sweet places
between your words
where my tongue probed.
I remember the brass clash
of cymbals
when your tongue
struck my nipple
I remember the purple sounds
of your tongue in my cunt.
Your tongue was the bell clapper
to my bell.

I remember your tongue
which rolled out
like a red carpet.
I remember your plushy royal purple
velvet tongue.
I remember your Nazi tongue

which hummed Wagner.
I remember your light & playful
Mozart tongue.

This poem is a gob of spittle,
a thin dribble.
It meant to speak all tongues,
it meant to sing.
But yours is in my mouth
& I am dumb.

The house of the body
is a stately manor
open for nothing
never to the public.

But
for the owner of the house,
the key-holder—
the body swings open
like Ali Baba's mountain
glistening with soft gold
& red jewels.

These cannot be stolen
or sold for money.
They only glisten
when the mountain opens
by magic
or its own accord.

The gold triangle of hair,
its gentle *ping*,
the pink quartz crystals
of the skin,
the ruby nipples,
the lapis
of the veins
that swim the breast . . .

The key-holder
is recognized
by the way he holds
the body.
He is recognized
by touch.

Touch is the first sense to awaken
after the body's little death
in sleep.
Touch is the first sense
to alert the raw red infant
to a world of pain.

The body glimmers
on its dark mountain
pretending ignorance of this.

The Cabala According to
Thomas Alva Edison

All objects give off sparks

Your tongue, for example, enters my mouth
& sends electricity along my veins

When we embrace in your office, your secretary turns blue
As the base of a flame

Your fly zips up & down making the sound
of a struck match

Even a struck match gives off sparks

My nails on the back of your knees
give off sparks
your nails on my thighs

Thighs, in general, give off sparks
But even the fuzz on thighs
gives off sparks

Sparks, in general, make the world go round
(There are, for example, spark plugs)

Plugs, in general, give off sparks

In & Out: the current of the world

The first snow of the year
& you lying between my breasts
in my husband's house
& the snow gently rising in my throat
like guilt,
& the windows frosting over
as if etched by acid.

You come from the desert
& have left a little sand
between my legs
where it rubs & rubs
& secretes a milky fluid,
finally a poem
or a pearl.

I am your oyster shell,
your mother of pearl
gleaming like oil on water
for two hours on a snowy day.

"Poets fall in love to write about it!"
I said in my brittle way,
& told you about other loves to tempt you
& heard your siren songs of old affairs.

I fall in love as a kind of research project.
You fall in love as some men go to war.

What tanks!
What bombs!
What storms of index cards!

I am binding up your legs with carbon ribbon.
I tie you to the bed with paper chains.

I am in love with my womb
& jealous of it.

I cover it tenderly
with a little pink hat
(a sort of yarmulke)
to protect it from men.

Then I listen for the gentle *ping*
of the ovary:
a sort of cupid's bow
released.
I'm proud of that.
& the spot of blood
in the little hat
& the egg so small
I cannot see it
though I pray to it.

I imagine the inside
of my womb to be
the color of poppies
& bougainvillea
(though I've never seen it).

But I fear the barnacle
which might latch on
& not let go
& I fear the monster
who might grow

to bite the flowers
& make them swell & bleed.

So I keep my womb empty
& full of possibility.

Each month
the blood sheets down
like good red rain.

I am the gardener.
Nothing grows without me.

Going to School in Bed

If it is impossible to promise
absolute fidelity,
this is because
we learn so much geography
from the shifting of one body
on another.

If it is impossible to promise
absolute fidelity,
this is because
we learn so much history
from the lying of one body
on another.

If it is impossible to promise
absolute fidelity,
this is because
we learn so much psychology
from the dreaming of one body
of another.

Life writes so many letters
on the naked bodies of lovers.
What a tattoo artist!
What an ingenious teacher!

Is it any wonder we appear
like schoolchildren dreaming:
naked
& anxious to learn?

I put our books face to face
so they could talk.
They whispered about us.

I put yours on top of mine.
They would not mate.

Like poor dumb pandas in the London Zoo,
they would not come together.

I put them back to back.
They would not sleep.

I put them right side up to upside down.
They would not lick each other's wounds.

The night we met
you fed me fish eggs & dark beer.
We spoke of animals & Shakespeare.
You talked about acidic inks & papers.
You told me how our books digest themselves.

You laid the pages of your body over mine.
You printed my face with kisses.
The letters fell into a heap under the bed.
The sheets were dust.
The fish eggs swam our mouths.

I thought that by going away
I would keep you.
I would fill myself up
with your absence.
My legs would close
around the smell of you.
My tongue would probe
the rainy air
& the whole sky
would be your mouth
& Hampstead Heath your tongue
& I face down
upon the grass
would tongue the sodden ground
& taste you there.

Instead,
I am on a plane
moving away from you.
The minutes sound
like jet-screams in my ears.
The hours lower into place
like landing gear.
We turn & bank
(the engines are my heart)
& we are in New York.

Dr. Love,
I thought you'd cure me.
I was lying on the couch
holding your hand.

You told me fear
was my disease.
& look—
I have been analyzed for years
& still
it brings me down.

Come back!
(I can say this having left you.)
We'll fuck so hard the world
will fall apart.

Your pink tongue's in my mouth.
It speaks for me.
I love this sickness more than life.
There is no cure.

What will the lovers *do* with their letters?
All night they lie awake scribbling
on each other's brains,
collecting lines they have no place to keep,
collecting memories which dip & flutter
like the moth of his tongue
in her cunt's flame.

They send each other letters—
telepathic letters, notebook letters,
muttered subway letters,
love words offered on the toilet seat,
love words spoken to a spoon or pot,
love words spoken to a dog,
a husband even,
love words scattered everywhere
but where they mean to go.

The lovers need a go-between.
Sometimes all of life comes down
to the search for a go-between.

She is writing on the air
above her husband's head.
He is scratching his wife's ass
& writing to her.
The air is full of letters, letters, letters!

Western Union, Eastern Union—what can join them?
Not even telephones can save them,
nor the persistence of mailmen in rain & fog & sleet.
Their lives are letters which they cannot send.
Their love has no address.

Because she loved her husband
she found a lover.
Because she betrayed her husband with false fidelity
she went to bed with her lover.
Because she was no longer falsely faithful
she now felt honest.
Because she was honest
she told her lover she loved him.
Because she was honest
she told her lover she also loved her husband.
Because she was honest
her dishonest lover left her.
Because her lover left her
she felt betrayed.
Because she felt betrayed
she went back to her husband.
Now they had something in common.

Eve on Riverside Drive

When they wrenched you
from my side—

my curved rib,
my bone,
my beauty—

it was as if the sun
were gouged from the sky
& the clouds
ran red.

A common sunset
over Riverside Drive.
Eden in smog.
The industrial wastes
of New Jersey,
the apartment towers of the Mafia,
the thick vaseline
of the sky.

& I aching
with loneliness
as if I had just had
an abortion
& you thousands of miles away.

They told the story
the other way around
(Adam forfeits rib;

Eve is born)—
Obvious irony.
Everyone knew
that women do the bearing;
men are born.

Juvenal God
writing the Bible
with his poison pen.

Cross out the lie!
Correct the blasphemy!

They wrenched you
from my side.
My blood poured down.
We both were born.
The pain belonged to me.

Sadder

Because I was sadder than you
to start with
I loved harder.

When I'm alone in my room
the objects breathe
like patients in a ward
for contagious diseases.

When I'm alone at night
the white ceiling presses down on me
like an iceberg
& brown leaves move like mice
under the bed.

You putter in your garden.
You are painting the prow of a boat
to launch on the Thames.
You are grinding coffee by hand
or lying under your car
as if under a woman.

Cooking or fucking,
you live in your skin.

I wander the world like an exile
& occasionally rest
on the shores of a poem.

But you were happier shoveling shit
than I was writing a poem

& that was hard.
I wanted to give up words
& stay with you.

I wanted to try.

But my sadness
was a stern husband.
He would not give me
a divorce.

Sleeptalk

Our dreams rise above our heads
& embrace

They ride together
in the ghostly trains of light
which streak across the ceiling

We sleep in their wake

A thin river of slime
joins our snail-mouths

Our eyelids twitch
the Morse codes
of our dreams

Our fingers clutch & unclutch
at the darkness

Palm upward to the stars
mouths shaping zeros
to the silence

Your penis rising
to conduct
your dreams

My moving tongue
still singing to itself

Nights we spend apart
I am at the bottom of a lake
with my loneliness.
Even a fishhook
would taste good.
I throw myself a line.
I write.

Night terrors come back.
I am four.
There is a man under the bed
who holds his breath
so I will think he's dead.
I know he's cheating
& I hold mine too.
We wait each other out.

Last gasp.
The water fills my lungs.
WOMAN KILLED BY DROWNING IN HER DREAMS.

At the bottom of the world
where books dissolve,
when pencils turn to salt,
where Venice sinks
under the weight
of stolen gold,
the blind fish bump me
& I turn to them.

I speak their silent thoughts
before I sleep.

Three

The best lovers
think constantly of death.
It keeps them honest.
It causes them to make love all night,
avoiding sleep.

We made love all night—
we three.
You & me
& that death's head
which slept between us.
The third impression on our pillow
was death itself—
& I smoothed back your moustache
in the direction from which
it had grown.

All night you drank from me.
The light was bone white,
moon white, white as gravestones.
The sheets were limestone,
the blankets marble shrouds
& in the morning
we lay there quite as numb
as a sarcophagus king
& queen.

What a loving corpse you were!
I have known living men
to be much, much colder.

Being dead,
we needed so much heat—
that we rubbed each other's flints
& made blue sparks.

I think how valiantly we fought off sleep,
& of your skin
like worn-down marble.

I think especially of your gentleness.
Death also can be thanked
for that.

For a Marriage

(seven years old, just beginning)

After we had torn out
each other's ribs
& put them back—

after we had juggled thigh bones
& knee caps,
& tossed each other's skulls at friends,

after we had sucked
each other's blood
& spat it out,

after we had sucked
each other's blood
& swallowed it
licking our lips—

after the betrayals
& imagined betrayals—

after you left me in the snow
& I left you in the rain
& we both came back—

after staying together
out of lust
& out of fear
& out of laziness—

we find ourselves
entangled in each other's arms,
grown into each other
like Siamese twins,
embedded in each other
like ingrown toenails,

& for the first time
wanting each other
only.

IV / SLEEPING WITH DEATH

*. . . melancholia is about as happy a state
as any other, I suppose.*

ZELDA FITZGERALD

*I sing of autumn and the falling fruit
and the long journey towards oblivion.*

*The apples falling like great drops of dew
to bruise themselves an exit from themselves.*

D. H. LAWRENCE

The cage of myself clamps shut.
My words turn the lock.

I am the jailor rattling the keys.
I am the torturer's assistant
who nods & smiles
& pretends not
to be responsible.

I am the clerk who stamps
the death note
affixing the seal, the seal, the seal.

I am the lackey who "follows orders."
I have not got the authority.

I am the visitor
who brings a cake, baked
with a file.

Pale snail,
I wave between the bars.
I speak of rope with the hangman.
I chatter of sparks & currents
with the electrician.
Direct or alternating,
he is beautiful.

I flatter him.
I say he turns me on.

I tell the cyanide capsules
they have talent

& may fulfill themselves someday.
I read the warden's awful novel
& recommend a publisher.
I sleep with the dietitian
who is hungry.
I sleep with the hangman
& reassure him
that he is a good lover.

I am the ideal prisoner.

I win prizes on my conduct.
They reduce my sentence.
Now it is only 99 years
with death like a dollop
of whipped cream at the end.
I am so grateful.

No one remembers
that I constructed this jail
& peopled its cells.
No one remembers my blueprints
& my plans,
my steady hammering,
my dreams of fantastic escapes.

& even I,
patiently writing away,
my skin yellowing
like the pages of old paperbacks,
my hair turning gray,
cannot remember the first crime,
the crime
I was born for.

The Lure of the Open Window
IN MEMORY OF JOEL LIEBER

Truth has very few friends and those few are suicides.
ANTONIO PORCHIA

The mouth of the night is open.
It wants to eat me.
It says the stars are lonely for me.
It lures me
with a faint wind
like a song.

This window
is the exit of the world.
Beyond it hover
my friends who have stepped off the earth,
out of themselves.
Like beginning swimmers,
they are treading air.

Why does the window
sing to me that way?

At the bottom of the pit
are alley cats & bottle glass
not truth.

Twenty windy stories down,
would I become
wholly myself?

The window hisses.

It is trying to blow out
this poem.

Is there no way out of the mind?
SYLVIA PLATH

Living in a death's head,
peering at life through its eyeholes,
she wondered why she could see only death,
why the landscape of clouds & mountains
looked to her
like the profiles of giant corpses
lying across
the horizon.

She lived in the skull.
She had always lived in the skull.
She kept it tidy.
She swept the floor of the jaw.
She dusted the ridge of the nose.
She rubbed
the nonexistent windows of the eyes
until they shone
like air.
Then she cooked lunch
& rested
on a molar.

Beyond the glittering rows of teeth
she saw the world:
everyone eating or being eaten.
She longed for a lover
to share her house & food
& make her feel alive.

Thirteen Lines for a Childless Couple

Because they thought always of the world ending
because he feared the whiplash of his father's sperm
because she feared the carriages & diapers
because she feared the splitting of her self
because she feared the world rushing in
because he studied little children

they never had children

Their child waited on skis at the top of a green hill
for the snowfall of his father's sperm

They huddled in the ski lodge drinking tea
& studying the cloud configurations

Eventually they died there

& the snow covered them

I am writing to you from the end of the world.
HENRI MICHAUX

Here, at the end of the world,
the flowers bleed
as if they were hearts,
the hearts ooze a darkness
like india ink,
& poets dip their pens in
& they write.

"Here, at the end of the world,"
they write,
not knowing what it means.
"Here, where the sky nurses on black milk,
where the smokestacks feed the sky,
where the trees tremble in terror
& people come to resemble them. . . ."

Here, at the end of the world,
the poets are bleeding.
Writing & bleeding
are thought to be the same;
singing & bleeding
are thought to be the same.

Write us a letter!
Send us a parcel of food!
Comfort us with proverbs or candied fruit,
with talk of one God.

Distract us with theories of art
no one can prove.

Here at the end of the world
our heads are empty,
& the wind walks through them
like ghosts
through a haunted house.

It is boring, this waiting for death.
Some days, the wind feathers your hair
& you open your mouth
on a wafer of sky
& you think of death as a book
with blue pages
which you will write.

You will write it by erasing
letter by letter
each word,
each endless day.

Meanwhile the boredom,
the vulgar fat novel:
your life.
Waiting for the baby to be born.
Waiting for the cast to come off,
& scribbling little poems on the plaster.

Where is the archway?
Where is the Tiepolo sky?
Where are the angels & putti?
Where is the life you are so afraid to lose?

They are the clean boys from the Midwest
who come to New York
with pennies on their tongues
to pay the piper.

They open their mouths & money tumbles out
this ought to be
negotiable for poems
but it is not.

Oh they are glib as pockets full of change
& all have girlfriends
& all turn on
& all get laid two times a week, at least,
& write about it.

They bring their poems to the man
who's slept with death,
& are baffled
when he laughs.

The Universal Explicator

The Universal Explicator
hums softly to itself
the names of dreams
separates the hungers
sets them against each other

The Universal Explicator
grinds out bullets with its bowels
speeches with its mouths
air pollution
from every pore

The Universal Explicator
even makes love
with a choice of dildoes
simultaneously makes war
simultaneously talks peace

The Universal Explicator
gives fellowships to bombs
& defense contracts to poets

A man once tried to murder it
His bullets boomeranged
& shot him dead
The Universal Explicator
canonized him instantly

The Universal Explicator
is tiny & fits
in the palm of your soul
If cornered will explode
inside you

The Other Side of the Page

I pass to the other side of the page.
PABLO NERUDA

On the other side of the page
where the lost days go,
where the lost poems go,
where the forgotten dreams
breaking up like morning fog,
go
go
go

I am preparing myself for death.

I am teaching myself emptiness:
the gambler's hunger for love,
the nun's hunger for God,
the child's hunger for chocolate
in the brown hours
of the dark.

I am teaching myself love:
the lean love of marble
kissed away by rain,
the cold kisses of snow crystals
on granite grave markers,
the soul kisses of snow
as it melts in the spring.

On the other side of the page
I lie making a snow angel

with the arcs
of my arms.

I lie like a fallen skier
who never wants to get up.

I lie with my poles, my pens
flung around me in the snow
too far to reach.

The snow seeps
into the hollows of my bones
& the calcium white of the page
silts me in like a fossil.

I am fixed in my longing for speech,
I am buried in the snowbank of my poems,
I am here where you find me

dead

on the other side of the page.

From the Country of Regrets

Those who live by the word will die listening.
DELMORE SCHWARTZ

It is a country where you can touch nothing: the food, the toilets, the people. The flies are everywhere. You come with your pockets stuffed with money, but there's nothing you can buy for fear of contamination, and nothing you can let touch you.

You enter a hotel with a central court. White plaster nymphs and cherubs in the fountain. Blue and yellow walls with white icing. Palms, ferns, growing out of white plaster planters. Servants sliding around noiselessly as if on invisible ball-bearings. Fans turning overhead. The constant continuo of the fountain in the central court. But the statues are sugar. Gradually, the water erodes them and they crumble and fall into the fountain. The fountain crumbles and falls into itself. The whole court dissolves. Next, it begins to dissolve the hotel and the guests, who are also made of sugar. The hawks circle and circle overhead, but they are not interested in melted sugar.

(*Directions to the Ruins*)

Where is the gate?

> It is a mouth with a tongue
> It is the curled tongue
> of the rain god

Where is the door?

> Under the eyes
> Behind the teeth
> kissed with moss

Where is the roof?

> Over the breasts
> Under the sky
> ruined

Where is the floor?

> Fragments
> A mosaic of a dolphin
> The lost poems of the dolphin minstrels

Where are the birds?

> Under the eaves
> Under the stones
> gone

Where is the altar?

> Under the throat
> Pitted with rain
> slick with blood

Where is the tower?

> Between your legs
> Above the hill
> falling

Where is the well?

> Filled with the bones of girls
> with gold   with blood
> dry

Where is the tomb?

> Follow the signs
> Across the river
> above you

The taxis in this country are ancient American cars. They start with a death rattle in the ignition. They puff along producing a great deal of noise and very little motion. Every thrust forward seems an immense effort. On hills, the drivers and passengers have to get out and push. These cabs are usually painted bright red or green. The paint-jobs are amateurish and seem hastily done to conceal the American paint underneath. Even the windshields are painted red or green. Only little slits remain for the drivers to look out. The interiors are covered everywhere possible with transparent red plastic. It hangs down in strips like old wallpaper. Glued to the plastic are amulets of all kinds: blue beads against the evil eye, Infants of Prague, fat-bellied Buddhas, Arabic mottoes, St. Christopher medals, homages to Quetzalcoatl, tiny reproductions of copulating Hindu gods, copies of the Lascaux animals, tiny plastic unicorns, griffins, sea dragons.

It is difficult to communicate with the people because every family speaks a different language, handed down through the generations and kept within the family like an heirloom. There are a few common words which the whole populace shares: words for MOTHER, MOUTH, FOOD, WAR; the verbs for MAKE, STEAL, BEAT, KILL. . . . But even these words have personal family equivalents which people use in their own homes. A complete common language is not necessary because incest is the rule in this country, and children mate with their own parents and never leave home. Their children, in turn, mate with them, and sometimes even with the grandparents when the grandparents are young enough. There are great numbers of deformed people and hemophiliacs as a result, and citizens with no birth defects are regarded with suspicion, as if they had some contagious disease.

(Chant at the Body's Birth-gate or the Nunnery-door)

Into the mouth

> lost lost forever
> & the teeth
> that prison

Into the eyes

> pull down the shades
> the brain still ticks

Into the nose

> hold it
> it stinks

Into the ears

> oh horny for music

Into the breasts

> dry as powdered bone

Into the navel

> flat
> no tunnel

Into the anus

> cities will die there

Into the cunt

> The cave of the mother
> let me lie down there
> rest
> let me rest

Tourists arrive in the country expecting a pleasant vacation, but within a few days, they are ready to leave. Generally, they fall prey to terrible diarrhea, or vomiting, or both. They try, despite their illness, to visit the great landmarks: The Temple of the Club-footed Virgin, The Cathedral of the Ebony Hermaphrodite, The Triumphal Arch built by King Akiliomoatli, who was born without arms or legs and invented a kind of primitive wheelchair called "doabo" which many citizens still use. But sightseeing is soon made impossible by the constant bouts of diarrhea and the fact that public toilets are either very scarce or contaminated. A few enterprising citizens have made themselves rich by building toilet booths near the main public attractions and charging exorbitant rates to desperate victims. The people who have gotten rich this way are both admired for their shrewdness and looked upon with contempt by the rest of the populace —rather the way Jews are looked upon by gentiles in our culture. Often they become quite influential, but they are never allowed full equality in government and civic positions, and from time to time they are purged in pogroms (called, oddly enough, "Regrets"—though it has no connection whatsoever with the English word, and has, in fact, a wholly different etymology). After these pogroms, the toilet booths are confiscated by the State and given to other citizens. These citizens then become part of the hated caste and in a few generations their descendants are purged, and so it goes. Tourists from our own country consider this horrifying and barbaric.

Invariably, tourists decide to leave after less than a week. They try to make plane reservations, but find the hotel staffs sullen and disinterested. The concierges shrug their shoulders and pretend not to understand when the tourists insist they want to leave. They go to the airline offices but find them always closed. They try to call, but none of the telephones work. Finally, in desperation, they pack and go to the airport.

The airport (which one scarcely noticed on arrival) proves to be one smallish room with peeling yellow walls, old American pop music (a woman singing ''Yes, We Have No Bananas'' and a man singing ''Teenie Weenie Bikini'' seem to be the only two records), fans turning overhead, and thousands upon thousands of mosquitoes. The wind riffles a five-year-old calendar with pictures of half-naked girls sitting on orange tractors.

A weathered sign labeled INFORMATION INFORMACION IN- FORMAZIONE hangs over what appears to be a counter. On closer inspection, one finds it is a bar, and those glittering objects which promised so much information are really liquor bottles.

An old woman walks by carrying a pillow in a soiled pillow- case. Except for her, everyone is in straw hats and sunglasses and leis and everyone is overburdened with piñatas, cameras, bottles of watered-down scotch, straw baskets, reproductions of ancient amphorae, straw flowers, skin-diving gear, guide- books, and pornographic postcards showing leathery-skinned peasant women fornicating with bored-looking donkeys be- fore the ruins. Because of the mosquitoes, everyone is scratch-

ing ankles, knees, wrists. There is always a high whine in the
air around one's ears.

(*The Poem About Ruins*)

It is your life which writes
the poem about ruins

              :

         It rises purple
         as a plumed serpent
         on a jungle coast

Its eyes are green

       :

        the veined wings
        of green insects

It worships sun

      :

        We are sitting our adolescence out
        here on the damp floor of a tomb

        We lie praying our hands like buried kings
        Moss kisses our genitals & lips

The poem about ruins
is inside us
trembling

      :

        It turns our cheeks
        slate blue

No one,
it tells us,
can write it

Blank sun

I rest on the crumbled wall
of Caracalla's Baths

Something has dried the water up!

A butterfly lights on one shoulder wing

A Roman boy
would like to scrub my back

But my head is parched

                    :

                    The poem about ruins

We stumble through the labyrinth in Crete

Here Theseus fell
& Ariadne spread her legs
Here jars of honey stood
here jars of oil
a small way off
there stood the jars of bones

            Weeds sprouted from the furrows in my brow
            Rain pitted all the limestone of my cheeks
            The paint washed off as off the Parthenon
            My navel filled with earth

We are sifting through the stones
Ephesus, perhaps, or Ostia

Somewhere near some sea

There is a statue of my mother here
My father is the snake twined round her waist

                                        Look down!

            We are climbing the Magician's Temple in Uxmal
            You cannot count steps up to the sun

            We cling because we want to fall
            & the poem about ruins
            will be lost

Suddenly, everyone is herded into line for Customs and inter-
rogated severely. A number of people are made to pay the last
of their money as duty on articles they brought with them.
They argue with the officials, but they cannot prove owner-
ship and, in desperation, they pay. When they return to their
seats, some girls find that their pornographic postcards have
been stolen. They want to complain to the authorities, but
cannot remember any of the words for "donkey."

Finally, the plane is heard landing. The passengers all run
out to see it taxi up to the gate. It is a sorry specimen: an
old propeller plane with only three working engines and no
familiar markings. It bears a painted Dodo on its flank and
an Eohippus on its somewhat dented tail. Several of the
women become hysterical and refuse to board. Children begin
to cry. "Teenie Weenie Bikini" is still playing.

The crew walks out smartly. The captain appears to be wearing a black cowboy suit from a 1940s Western, and a black mask, silver spurs and six-shooters. The stewardesses are dressed like dance hall girls of the Old West. They go over to the INFORMATION bar and order double bourbons which they proceed to bolt down. All the passengers watch them as they parade back across the room and out to the plane.

There is much reluctance and shuffling around, but everyone finally boards. The old woman with the pillow is seen boarding last. The mechanics do a vaudeville imitation of checking the engines, but the fact that they are really not doing anything is clear. One propeller is still not working properly. It turns sluggishly. The takeoff is as slow as running in a dream. The plane seems to hover for a long time with its tail grazing the runway, and the tire treads screech at the moment of takeoff. Then, miraculously, the plane is aloft and hovering over the ocean. The seatbelt sign is still on. The pilot's voice is heard over the P.A. system: "Due to mechanical failure, we will crash shortly." The passengers sit riveted to their seats. Some laugh raucously. Others scream for the stewardesses. Others order drinks.

(*Invisible, with Stalled Engines*)

Perhaps we are not sinking
but God is going higher

He is finally invisible

Clouds pass above us
like milk in water

The sky is water

The plane we fly in
is a giant fish
which seems to stand still

But we believe in motion
we believe in the idea of motion

Forward, we say, is where
we are going

Perhaps God is going higher

We are not sinking
We do not believe we are sinking

Some young people are heard begging the stewardess for philo-
sophical explanations. What have they done wrong? Why
does evil have to exist? Why does death? Who willed it all?
Doesn't the captain have any power over it?

The stewardesses bat their false eyelashes and smile their
plastic smiles and ask: "Milk or juice, sir?" Other passengers
sit paralyzed, listening for messages in the sound of the
engines. They believe their hearts and the engines correspond.

And there in the corner, writing about everyone, trying to
separate herself out of the scene, or be above it, or control it,
or pretend she dreamed it—am I. I am the one with the open
notebook, the one who lost her pornographic postcards, the
one with thousands of mosquito bites behind each knee. Noth-

ing bad can happen to me. I am only collecting material. I am making notes: on hell, on heaven.

It seems as though we have been waiting hours for the crash, but this may be an illusion. The stewardesses have not served drinks yet. Perhaps they do not intend to because of the mechanical trouble. One cannot tell. Also, one cannot hear the engines for the singing. Strapped in our seats, suspended above the ill-fitting fragments of our lives, we are singing. There is no place to get to. The sun is setting below the horizons of our eyes, and all our windows seem to be on fire.

To the Reader

At the point X
the point of ignition,
the point where one tick
of the clock
joins with another,
the point where the scratch of the match
bursts into flame—

that is where I begin,
where I open my hand
to the reader
& shake out my cuffs,
where I show my magician's hat
& swear on my life
it is empty.

At the moment of impact,
at blast-off plus one,
my acetylene pencil
is searing my name
on the backs of my lovers,
my fountain pen breaks into blossom . . .
the paper is pooling with rain.

At the stroke of lightning—
when Toledo appears as a gleam
in El Greco's eye—

at the clap of thunder—
when Beethoven goes deaf
& invents the ear—

I am trying to learn
to begin to begin to begin.

ABOUT THE AUTHOR

ERICA JONG was born in New York City and educated at Barnard and Columbia. Her first book of poems, *Fruits & Vegetables,* was published in 1971. She has won *Poetry* magazine's Bess Hokin prize, *New York Quarterly*'s Madeline Sadin award, a grant from the New York State Council on the Arts, and the Alice Fay di Castagnola award of the Poetry Society of America (for *Half-Lives*).

Ms. Jong lives and writes in Manhattan, where she also teaches a poetry workshop at the 92nd Street Y. Her poems have appeared in several anthologies, including *The Best Poems of 1971* and *Fifty Modern American and British Poets,* and many magazines, including *Harper's, The Nation, Mademoiselle, Ms., The Paris Review, Columbia Forum, Cosmopolitan, Poetry, The American Poetry Review,* among others. She is currently at work on a novel.